PRAY WITHOUT CEASING

For the Most Rev. Dr Rowan Williams,
Archbishop of Canterbury
with grateful thanks for his ministry,
his wisdom and spirituality,
his humility and for his loving support
and encouragement.

Jenny Child

Pray without Ceasing

the columba press

First edition, 2012, published by
the columba press
55A Spruce Avenue, Stillorgan Industrial Park,
Blackrock, Co. Dublin

Cover by Bill Bolger
Origination by The Columba Press
Printed by MPG Books Group Ltd.

ISBN 978 1 85607 857 3

Introduction

Prayer is the cry of our hearts to God. It needs to be natural and sincere. It should not just be words, but should be an offering of the heart, mind and soul to God. We need to be still before our Creator. So often we come with a 'shopping list' of requests, rather than being ready to listen and respond to what the Lord is seeking to say to us. The prayers in this book are written in the hope of giving readers thoughts or topics to be used as they desire. It is my prayer that these prayers will be a blessing to many.

Jenny Child

Foreword

Jenny Child has created a really valuable resource for our daily prayer with this lovely book *Pray without Ceasing*. I am very conscious in the Cathedral here in Canterbury of how important the rhythm of prayer is as we are called regularly together in the morning and in the evening. The prayers which are set for us undergird those which spring from our hearts and minds and they prompt a life of prayer which we ourselves create from our own experiences and relationship with God day by day. This book with its simple prayer for each day of the year gives that rhythm even for those with very busy lives. It is of course a treasure house of prayers that can be used on any day of the year but its most valuable contribution to our life of prayer will be the foundation stone of prayer which it gives to each day and on which we can build creatively. I very much hope that *Pray without Ceasing* will be used by very many people to enrich their lives and to lead them more deeply into a relationship with the God who loved us so much that he gave himself to us in the person of Jesus Christ who taught his disciples to pray.

Robert Willis,
Dean of Canterbury

January

1 January

God of new beginnings,
a new year stretches before us –
untouched, fresh – with all its possibilities.
Give us the spirit of adventure
that we may dare new things for you.
May we know that you walk the road with us,
in joy and in sorrow.
Fill us with courage to enter this new year –
this next stage of our pilgrimage –
knowing that you are with us.

2 January

God the Creator,
you made us,
God the Son,
you died for us,
God the Holy Spirit,
you make us holy.
Father, Son and Holy Spirit,
bless, preserve and protect us
that wherever we go or whatever we do,
it may be according to your will.

3 January

God of judgement as well as mercy,
each one of us will have to stand
before you one day, to give account of our lives –
our deeds and our words.
May we hear the words, 'Well done,
good and faithful servant.'

4 January

Lord, you created infinite beauty
and diversity from nothing.
May we appreciate the sheer scale
of your abundant creation.
May we guard it and preserve it
ensuring that all creatures are treated
with care and respect.

5 January

In our striving, Lord,
Guide us,
In our living, Lord,
Direct us,
In our travelling, Lord,
Protect us,
And at journey's end,
Lord, receive us.

6 January

We give thanks
for all that has been,
for all that is yet to be,
for the gift of this new day.
May we use it to your glory, dear Lord
and may we commit the unknown future
into your hands.

7 January

Lord, you call us to follow you,
give us the resolve.
You ask for our faithfulness,
make us steadfast.
You demand our obedience,
give us that willingness
to be your disciple.

8 January

O God, touch our lives with your glory
that we may reach out to others.
Fill our hearts with your love
that all may see the love of Christ in us.
Inspire us to take on new endeavours for you
that we may encourage those without hope.
Open our lives to your Spirit
that we may reflect your praise.

9 January

Peace to neighbour,
Peace to friend,
Peace to each nation,
Peace to the world,
Peace in my heart.
O, Prince of Peace,
may your kingdom come.

10 January

Lord, you touch our lives
with the gentleness of your love,
you inspire in us everything
that is good and pure,
help us to walk in your way
and bring glory to your name.

11 January

My soul longs for peace, for stillness
for quietness, for a cessation of voices,
for silence –
just to wait upon you, my God.

12 January

May the Seeking One, find you,
May the Welcoming One, receive you,
May the Redeeming One, save you,
May the Loving One, fill you,
May the Guiding One, lead you,
May the Living One, renew you,
May the Rejoicing One, delight you,
May the Grieving One, comfort you,
May the Protecting One, hold you,
And may Father, Son and Holy Spirit
bless you, each day, each night.

13 January

Lord God, I don't know where I'm going
I cannot see the way ahead,
The future's door is closed to me –
It is enough for me,
To trust your leading,
To feel your presence,
And to know that you are there
with me wherever I go.

14 January

Lord, draw near to us,
When we are betrayed by friends,
Undermined by colleagues,
And misunderstood by those we rely upon.
Be our strong tower,
Our refuge and our strength –
Our unfailing Friend.

15 January

God of grace and mercy,
You give us life,
You give us hope,
You give us opportunity –
To serve you,
To encourage others.
Lord, here I am,
Use me according to your will.

Pray without Ceasing

16 January

Lord, before I speak
help me to ask myself,
Is it kind?
Is it true?
Is it necessary?
Touch my lips with your love,
that what I say might please and glorify you.

17 January

May the power of the presence
surround us,
May the strength of your love
enfold us,
May the fire of your Spirit
fill us,
That we may live to your glory, O God.

18 January

You won't let me fall, Lord,
You won't let me down,
For underneath me
are your everlasting arms.
May I just rest in you.

19 January

As I rise from sleep,
May I live this day to your glory,
As I wash, cleanse me,
As I dress, clothe me with righteousness,
As I eat breakfast,
May I remember the hungry,
As I take my dog for a walk,
May I give thanks for your creation,
As I iron the clothes,
May I pray for all the troubled places
in the world,
As I visit friends,
May I think of the lonely and the unloved.
Lord, help me to show your love
not by my words alone
but by deeds of kindness.

20 January

God of all comfort,
Draw near to those
in grief, in sickness,
in despair,
those at their 'wits' end'.
You alone know their need.
May they find you will stand by them
in their hour of need.

21 January

O God, you are without beginning
and without end.
You brought me to birth,
be with me on my earthly pilgrimage
and at my departing.

22 January

Almighty God, you created everything from nothing.
We give thanks for the sun to warm us by day,
For the stars to guide us by night,
For the seasons in their diversity,
For water to give us life, we give thanks,
For rivers and oceans,
For deserts and rainforests,
For mountains and valleys,
For all plants and animals,
For all that you have made,
We give you thanks.

23 January

Lord, inspire my thinking,
Direct my doing,
Bless my speaking,
Guide my coming and my going,
Be with me whether
waking or sleeping,
each day, each night.

24 January

From hardness of heart,
Lord, be saving me,
From judging too harshly,
Lord, be keeping me,
From seeking the best place,
Lord, be sparing me.
Give me an open-hearted spirit
that I may try to love and not to judge,
give me lowliness of heart to work
for the betterment of others.

25 January

Loving Shepherd, you lead us
and go before us, guiding us.
You carry us on your shoulders
through the rough places of life.
You refresh us and let us rest
in lush green pastures.
You surround us with
a shepherd's tender care.
You comfort us when
we are hurting.
You hold us and love us,
because you are the Good Shepherd.

26 January

Lord, I want to be an island
Cut off by the tide,
Or a castle with a moat
And drawbridge lifted high.

Lord, I want to shut myself away
From the stress of daily life,
And spend some time in pastures green,
Far from the toil and strife.

But, you call me to be open
To all this day's demands,
And leave whate'er the future holds
Entirely in your hands.

27 January

O God, my heart is cold – so judgemental,
So ready to find fault.
Come with the warmth of your love
And light a fire within me.

Pray without Ceasing

28 January

God of abundant bounty,
Help us to care for the world,
May we not pollute the environment,
May we share the earth's resources fairly,
May we not exploit creation,
For we are stewards of your bounty –
It is a trust from you.

29 January

God of power and might,
your hand is still stretched out to heal
and bind up our wounds.
Look upon each one with your favour
that we may know the assurance
of your presence surrounding us,
above us, under us and within us.

30 January

God of light, shine in the dark places
of my life.
There are no secrets hidden from you
and you know the thoughts of all hearts.
I am ashamed of what you see
when you look into my heart.
Lord, cleanse my thoughts
that I may serve you worthily.

31 January

Even when the days are darkest,
You are with me, O Lord,
May I rest in you and patiently wait
for the fulfilment of your will in my life.

1 February

Lord, in the 'hubbub' of daily life,
help me to draw aside for moments
of reflection and refreshment.
May I be still and know
that you are God –
Just to be still –
Just to know,
You are God, my God.

2 February

Almighty God, judge us with mercy
not according to our deeds.
Forgive us our sins
because of your Son's death for us on the Cross.
Remember we are frail creatures of dust.
Look with pity on your Creation.

3 February

Lord, refuel our cold hearts with love,
rekindle the embers of enthusiasm
for our faith which we once had.
Fill us anew with the power of your Spirit
that our lives may be ablaze with your love
and that all may see Christ in us.

4 February

Lord, we ask for –
Peace instead of war,
Food instead of hunger,
Love instead of hate,
Generosity instead of greed,
Simplicity instead of materialism,
Truth instead of lies,
A just sharing of the earth's resources
And a willing heart to allow change to begin in me.

5 February

Lord Jesus, you calmed the sea,
you walked on water,
be the pilot of my boat,
as I face the storms of life.
Help me, just to trust you
to take the rudder and guide
my course wherever you will.

6 February

Risen Lord, thank you for those
I have loved in this life,
who are now at rest in your care.
They are now free from pain
and in your loving arms.
Comfort me, when I feel
bereft of their presence.
Thank you for the communion of saints –
that mystical link between
earth and heaven.

7 February

Fill our mouths with your message,
Set our feet on the right path,
Fix our minds on your Word,
Guide our hands by your will,
Open our hearts to your love,
That our lives may glorify you.

8 February

Love to neighbour,
Love to friend,
Love to foe,
Love to dear ones, near and far,
Love to everyone I meet.
Fill my heart with love, O God.

9 February

Lord of light and glory,
all majesty is yours
and all wisdom and power,
yet you care for us –
for each individual.
Not even a tiny sparrow
falls to the earth
without your knowing it,
such assurance is so wonderful,
I cannot understand it,
but I know it is true.

10 February

God of joy, you have given us
an abundance of all that is good.
Yet so often our faces are gloomy
and our lives joyless.
Stir up in us a fountain
of unadulterated joy
that your Spirit might flow from us
bubbling like a geyser from the warm earth.

11 February

O God, touch our hearts with generosity
that we may be willing to share
the world's wealth with those in poverty.
Food for those who are hungry,
clothing for those who are naked
and shelter for those who have none.
As we have freely received
from your bountiful abundance,
so may we freely give.

12 February

Lord of life and love,
we pray for the world
in all its brokenness.
May peace overcome war,
may love overcome hate,
may generosity overcome greed,
may gentleness overcome pride,
that the earth may be filled
with your glory, your peace.

13 February

We thank you for –
A new day,
A new page,
A new chapter,
In the journey of our lives.
Lead us, onward, heavenly Father
to our ultimate goal.

14 February

Lord, you cover the night sky
with a roll of black velvet
scattered with diamonds.
The stars are numberless, yet you count each one.
Who are we that we should matter to you?
So insignificant, yet you care for us and call us by name,
your love is infinite and beyond our understanding.

15 February

God be in my thinking,
God be in my hearing,
God be in my speaking,
God be in my waking,
God be in my sleeping,
Now and evermore.

16 February

You bear us up on eagles' wings.
Your arms are under us,
around us,
above us.
May we just trust ourselves
to your unfailing love, O Lord.

17 February

O God, you are my only hope.
My enemies consort together
to cause me trouble –
to bring me grief, without a cause.
Why have friends turned against me?
O God, be my defence and advocate.

18 February

Lord, help us to build on rock not on sand.
When life's storms prevail,
keep our faith firm.
When disappointments come,
keep our faith firm.
When illness strikes,
keep our faith firm.
When temptation assails,
keep our faith firm.
May we build our lives on you, our Rock.

19 February

Thank you, Lord, for dealing so graciously with me –
for your patience and mercy.
May I respond to your love
and seek to have even the smallest spark
of your divine love to share with others.

20 February

Whatever task I do – menial or profound –
let it be for your glory.
May I not think any job is beneath my dignity,
but rather, like you, dear Lord,
help me to assume the servant role willingly.

21 February

For the sun to warm us,
We give thanks, O Lord,
For the moon to direct us,
We give thanks, O Lord,
For the stars to guide us,
We give thanks, O Lord,
For the rain to refresh us,
We give thanks, O Lord,
For the breeze to cool us,
We give thanks, O Lord,
For your Spirit to fill us,
We give thanks, O Lord.

22 February

Bountiful God, you long for a world
that cares and shares –
fairly,
equitably,
consistently.
Help us to work for a just apportioning
of the earth's resources,
for honest dealing in all areas of daily living
and a generous spirit
to share what you have given us.

23 February

Lord, infiltrate the hidden recesses
of my heart
where long-harboured grudges
and resentments dwell.
Come with your cleansing power
and make me whole.

February

24 February

You shepherd us through the rough places,
you bear us on your shoulders.
When I feel weak,
help me not to fight you, Lord Jesus,
but just to trust you in complete surrender.

25 February

Lord, the sea of life is rough and deep
and I feel so insignificant – so vulnerable.
Pilot my little craft,
that finally after all the storms of life,
I may anchor in the heavenly port.

26 February

Creator God, you made all things
and saw your work was good.
Help us to cherish and respect your creation.
May we seek to prevent cruelty to and abuse of animals.
Save us from exploiting or overworking them.
May we realise they have feelings and experience pain.
You made us to share this planet with them in harmony.
Help us never to betray their trust.

27 February

Gracious God, you go before us,
You are with us,
you will be with us,
you will not fail us nor forsake us.
We give thanks for this assurance.

28 February

Everlasting God, your treasury overflows
with all that is good and lovely,
give us a portion of your compassion,
your love, that we might surrender
to your holy will and walk in your way.

29 February

Where there is despair, bring hope,
Where there is sickness, bring healing,
Where there is hunger, bring sustenance,
Where there is war, bring peace,
And all for your love's sake,
We pray, O God.

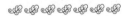

March

1 March

Widen our blinkered vision
with new glimpses of your glory.
Open our world-weary minds
to the freshness of your Spirit.
Soften our cynical hard-heartedness
with your expansive love.
Unfetter the preconceived ideas
which bind us,
that we may live in your glorious freedom.

2 March

God of all time and space,
one day is as a thousand years to you
and a thousand years as a day.
You give to each of us
a span of life – sometimes very short,
for others, many years.
May we use our lives, whether long or short,
to your glory.

3 March

You call us, Lord, to come apart
from the world and rest a while.
We are weary, we are burdened with life.
Refresh us with your loving care
and help us to go on in your strength.

4 March

Bountiful God, you have given us so much.
May we be faithful stewards
in the care of our planet.
We acknowledge our responsibility,
For our part in causing climate change,
We acknowledge our responsibility,
For the depletion of fish stocks in rivers and seas,
We acknowledge our responsibility,
For our careless consumption of energy,
We acknowledge our responsibility,
For the extinction of many species,
We acknowledge our responsibility,
For the misuse of resources,
We acknowledge our responsibility,
For polluting and exploiting your creation,
We acknowledge our responsibility
and ask your forgiveness.

5 March

I am in pain, Lord,
and I'm feeling tired.
Bear me up on eagles' wings
and renew my strength,
that I might run and not be weary,
and walk and not faint.

6 March

Give us the vision to see,
The clarity to hear,
The enthusiasm to act,
And the willingness to obey, O Lord.

March

7 March

Be my Shepherd, Lord, and lead me
in the pastures green,
Beside the still waters of reflection,
For there I need nothing,
Except the knowledge that you are with me,
Guiding me through the rough places of life,
Even in the dark vale of death itself.
You spread a table of refreshment for me
and make me welcome with the oil of comfort
anointing my soul.
Without a doubt you will walk with me
and lead me into your own home.

8 March

In our thinking, inspire us,
In our planning, direct us,
In our doing, support us,
In everything we undertake,
Be with us and guide us, loving Lord.

9 March

Lord, so often I've been impatient
for the future to come,
and now I long for the past –
for better days, or so I imagine.
Help me to be grateful
for the present – your gift –
and to use it wisely.

10 March

God of love and light,
You warm us with your sunshine,
You bring hope into our lives,
You scatter the darkness from our path,
Shine on us, in your risen glory.

11 March

We thank you, dear Father,
For happy memories –
of childhood,
of loved ones, perhaps no longer with us,
of holidays enjoyed,
of pets past and present who have shared our lives,
of Christmases long gone,
of all that is good and beautiful in our lives.
May we remember and be thankful.

12 March

Forgive my harsh words, O God of love,
The unthinking remark that hurts,
The cutting reply that was better left unsaid,
The tongue – my tongue causes such trouble,
Yet it can glorify you.
Forgive my harsh words, O God of love.

13 March

God be in my living,
God be in my dying,
God be in my talking,
God be in my walking,
God be in my sleeping,
God be in my weeping,
God be in my caring,
God be in my sharing,
God be in my living,
God be in my dying.

14 March

Lord Jesus,
you opened wide your arms on the cross
to embrace all humanity.
Draw us near with the cords of love
that we may know you more clearly,
love you more dearly
and follow you more nearly
day by day.

15 March

God of music and harmony,
we pray for peace –
in our hearts,
in our lives.
Soothe our jangled nerves
with the sweetness of your love.
May the beauty of music flow through us
and fill us with new hope.

16 March

Out of the depths of despair,
I cry to you, O God,
Plead my cause against my enemies,
Come to me in your mighty power,
For I am weak and weary.

17 March

God above me,
God below me,
God on my left,
God on my right,
God in my speaking,
God in my looking,
God in my hearing,
God in my doing,
God in all things –
God in my life.

18 March

Lord, sometimes you seem so far away,
I feel that you are watching me
'from a distance' – so removed
from my problems and fears –
yet you are near to me.
Lord, I believe, take away my unbelief.

19 March

You come to us in bread and wine, O Lord,
To nourish us,
To sustain us,
To strengthen us for life's pilgrimage.
Feed us evermore, we pray,
O Bread of Heaven.

20 March

We leave our mark on the world just once –
One life, one opportunity.
Our life is fleeting –
A candle in the wind, easily extinguished –
long or short in time,
a life of service to you, Lord, and to others,
or a life selfishly frittered away on trivialities.
Lord, teach us to number our days
and save us from dying suddenly and unprepared.

21 March

God of the springtime,
You bring new life to birth.
God of the summertime,
You help us to blossom
into the people you want us to be.
God of the autumn,
You support us as the nights lengthen.
God of the winter,
You encourage us in spite of aches and pains,
to look for new life in the promise of spring.

22 March

Lord, use my hands this day to your glory –
to help and not to hurt.
Use my lips to tell of your love,
not to utter harsh words.
May the love of Christ shine out of me,
that I might show people Jesus.

23 March

Quiet music – the organ whispers softly,
A gossamer thread from earth to heaven,
Be still and know that you are God,
Be still and know – to surrender utterly to you, my God.

24 March

Lord Jesus, you bid us come to you,
For your yoke is easy and your burden light.
Look in love and pity on the oppressed,
the exploited,
the vulnerable,
those just taken for granted by family and friends.
May they cast their burden on you,
knowing that you care for them.

25 March

Lord God, you called blessed Mary
to be the mother of your Son,
to be the 'God-bearer'.
We give thanks for her willingness to obey.
Give us that same obedience to offer ourselves
to be used in accordance with your perfect plan.

26 March

God of creativity, we praise you for all
that enhances our lives and brings us pleasure –
for music, for art, for ballet and drama.
Inspire all artistes and craftspeople
who seek to use their talents to glorify you
and bless their endeavours.

27 March

Great Shepherd of your sheep,
we pray for your church throughout the world.
You called it to be a witness to your truth,
forgive our apathy and renew in us a sense of mission.
May both clergy and laity
shine as lights in a dark world,
for we are the body of Christ.

Pray without Ceasing

28 March

Lord, in my loneliness, be with me,
In my sickness, comfort me,
In my hopelessness, support me,
In my fears and frustrations,
share with me.

29 March

Lord Jesus, you took the children
into your arms and blessed them.
Look in love upon your little ones,
guard them and help them to reach maturity
determined to serve you.

30 March

God of the universe, we give thanks
for opportunities to travel –
especially to holy places,
to broaden our minds
and to learn more of your saints.
Inspired by their examples, may we seek to walk
in the footsteps of our blessed Saviour Jesus Christ.

April

31 March

Through the hours of darkness,
Be with us,
In times of wakefulness,
Support us,
When pain unsettles our sleep,
Relax us,
When fears and worries trouble our minds,
Be near to us.
May we rest in you, knowing that you alone
can make us dwell in safety.

1 April

Loving Lord, we remember loved ones no longer with us.
We pray for those separated by distance,
Those parted from us because of some quarrel
or misunderstanding.
You know our needs –
Comfort the bereaved,
Uphold those far away
and bring harmony to those who are troubled.

2 April

Merciful God, you carry us on eagles' wings
and bear us on your heart
when we are in grief and sorrow.
You too have known the pain of human suffering.
You comfort us as the One
who laid down your life for the sheep.

3 April

Risen Lord, even though I walk
through the valley of death and despair,
you are with me,
carrying your wayward sheep
on your strong shoulders,
thank you for this assurance.

4 April

Lord, you are the vine
into which we the branches are grafted.
Without your power we can do nothing worthwhile.
Help us to abide in you
that we might bear much fruit to your glory.

5 April

Come, Holy Spirit, into our lives
darkened by sin,
come with your cleansing power
and glorious light,
come, change us and send us out
to serve a world which cries out
for your transforming love.

6 April

Give us grace to follow you, Lord,
tenacity to hold firm
to the faith of Christ,
endurance to run the race
that is set before us,
and obedience to your will
in everything we do.

7 April

May the strength of God, uphold us,
May the love of God, fill us,
May the wisdom of God, teach us,
May the light of God, guide us,
May the truth of God, enlighten us,
May the grace of God, save us,
May the protection of God, guard us,
May the freedom of God, liberate us,
May the presence of God, surround us,
This day and every day.

8 April

Fan the dying embers of my faith, Lord God,
and kindle a flame within my cold heart into a blaze
that I might shine as a light in this dark world.

9 April

So often, Lord Jesus,
I want to set the other person right.
Help me to examine my own life carefully
before I try to correct others.
Inspire me to follow your blessed example
that at the last day
I may be found acceptable in your sight.

10 April

In our grieving, be cheering us,
In our ailing, be healing us,
In our praying, be hearing us,
In our living, be guiding us –
Each day, each night, dear Lord.

11 April

Creator God, you fashioned this world
to be full of beauty,
but we have spoiled it by greed,
exploitation and apathy.
Forgive us, and help us to feel
responsibility for its welfare.
May we conserve,
protect and cherish,
its diversity and fragility.

12 April

Lord, give us the power
to be gentle,
the strength to be meek,
that we may be Christ to others
and bring glory to your name.

13 April

God of the universe,
you called your Church to serve humanity
and to proclaim the gospel.
So often it is persecuted and condemned
and sometimes, we have to admit,
apathetic and complacent.
Fan the smouldering embers of our faith
into the fire of Pentecost
that we may be your faithful witnesses in the world.

14 April

Eternal God, we give thanks
for all those who have influenced
our lives for good,
those who are positive role models for us.
May we follow the example of your blessed Son, Jesus Christ.

15 April

For the sick, we ask for healing,
For the bewildered, we ask for guidance,
For the troubled, we ask for peace,
For the homeless, we ask for shelter,
For the wanderers, we ask for direction,
For the bereaved, we ask for comfort,
Lord, in your mercy, hear our prayer.

16 April

From danger, be shielding us,
From sin, be saving us,
From sickness, be keeping us,
From temptation, be guarding us,
From the snares of the devil,
be protecting us,
From sudden and unprepared death,
be sparing us.

17 April

Lord, you surround us with your presence,
You quieten us with your love,
You encourage us with your Word,
You nourish us with bread and wine,
You fill us with your Spirit,
Lord, evermore defend us.

Pray without Ceasing

18 April

May the power of your presence
pervade my life,
may your peace which is beyond
human understanding fill me,
may I have the assurance that you are with me,
help me to entrust everything to you, O Lord.

19 April

Though dawn breaks cheerless today
and billows of clouds envelope me
and troubles rise up like mountains
and the sun is hidden from view,
yet you are there, the great Encourager,
leading me with the warmth of your love,
the brightness of your Spirit.

20 April

Almighty God, we pray for the leaders of the nations.
May they have a genuine desire to work for peace,
a willingness to listen to what others have to say
and a real commitment
to govern with justice and integrity.
May they ever be mindful that they are accountable to you.

21 April

From trouble be saving us,
From sickness be keeping us,
From temptation be sparing us,
From evil be protecting us,
Lord, in your mercy, hear us.

April

22 April

Sometimes, O God of mercy,
I just want to crawl under a rock
and hide from the world.
I am filled with regrets for unfulfilled dreams,
for ambitions not realised,
for things not achieved.
Help me to be grateful for all you have given me
and help me to be satisfied.

23 April

Lord, touch our cold hearts with your love,
instil in us a real desire
to live in peace with one another.
May we strive to work for peace in our world,
and may your kingdom come.

24 April

Lord of infinite compassion,
may we embrace the flesh and blood
motherhood of Mary in our care for each other.
Help us to be tender and patient
in our dealings with each other.

25 April

O God, our help in ages past,
we give thanks for all those who have
given their lives in the service of freedom.
May we be faithful stewards of their sacrifice.
May we strive for peace –
personally, nationally, globally.

26 April

Creative God, you stretched out your hand
and made the world diverse and beautiful.
We have blighted your plan
and the whole creation suffers because of sin.
May we treat animals
with the kindness and respect they deserve
and seek to prevent cruelty.
Give us a real desire not to exploit or misuse your creation.

27 April

Lord, stir our hearts to seek you,
enliven our minds to know you,
open our ears to hear you,
grant us a glimpse of your glory
that we may feel the touch
of heaven on us.

28 April

O Servant-King, help me to serve.
May I be willing not to seek
preferment or the best place,
but rather to set aside my pride
and be a servant for your sake.

29 April

Time passes so quickly – the days, the months, the years.
Lord, help me to use the time given to me wisely
and to your glory.
We spend so little time on the world's stage,
however long we live.
Help us to leave something worthwhile behind
when our life on earth is finished.

May

30 April

Love for family,
love for friends – near and far,
love for neighbours,
love for those I find it difficult to like
let alone love,
love for those who find me hard to bear.
Therefore, give us love, O God.

1 May

O God, your handiwork has made
this world diverse and beautiful.
May we cherish its fragility
by our care of all that you have created.
It is a trust from you.

2 May

Lord Jesus, you graced the marriage feast at Cana
and turned water into wine.
We pray for all those about to be married,
may they seek your blessing on their union.
Give them patience with each other
and tenderness when sorrows come.
May they know the assurance of your love for them,
and may they seek to live for each other and for you.

3 May

May the sun warm your back,
May the stars light your path,
May the breeze cool your face,
And may God guide, keep
and encircle you with his love.

Pray without Ceasing

4 May

Creator God, you made us in your own image
yet we have blighted your perfect plan by our sin.
Forgive us for grieving your heart of love.
We give thanks for Christ's death on the Cross
to redeem us and save us
from the consequences of our sin.
May we seek to follow your Son's example
in all that we do and say.

5 May

Lord, so often we try to 'ring-fence' you
by setting our own parameters
for what you will do in our lives.
Forgive our presumption.
May we be more open to the working
of your Holy Spirit
and more accepting of your will for us.

6 May

Almighty God, we pray for all church leaders –
for bishops, priests and deacons.
Guide all those who have responsibility
for the welfare of your holy Church.
May both clergy and laity shine as lights
in a dark world and be faithful witnesses
to the gospel.

7 May

Lord, you make all things new,
you give us new opportunities,
new possibilities,
new beginnings.
May we use wisely all that you give us.

8 May

From hardness of heart,
Good Lord, deliver us,
From the hasty retort,
Good Lord, deliver us,
From lack of patience,
Good Lord, deliver us,
From mean-spiritedness,
Good Lord, deliver us,
From being self-centred,
Good Lord, deliver us,
From all things that would grieve your Spirit,
Good Lord, deliver us.

9 May

Be with those, loving Father,
who are waiting –
for news of a loved one,
for the result of medical tests,
for a job interview,
for the birth of a child,
for an important letter,
for a phone call,
for death.
May we be found watching and waiting
at your Second Coming.

Pray without Ceasing

10 May

Help me, my God to show people Jesus,
by my words and by my actions,
by the way I live and by my example.
May the love of Christ shine out of me
that people may see Jesus.

11 May

Lord of light, you illuminate this world
with the radiance of your presence –
sunlight,
starlight,
candlelight,
daylight,
moonlight,
firelight,
lamplight,
searchlight,
torchlight,
the lights on a Christmas tree,
all remind us that you are the Light of the World.

12 May

Lord, my thoughts are in a turmoil.
I keep forgetting things
and leaving jobs undone.
Clear my mind and take the stress from my life.
Help me to rest in your peace.

13 May

Loving Saviour, look with compassion
on all places ravaged by war.
Especially be with those who live in fear of their lives,
those who have lost loved ones,
those whose homes have been devastated,
those who have lost everything.
Holy Jesus, we ask that you will bind up
the wounds of your broken world
and encompass your creation
in your loving arms.

14 May

Lord, you are rest to the weary,
Healing to the sick,
Light to the lost,
Comfort to the sorrowful,
Friend to the lonely,
You are there in every circumstance.

15 May

I stand within this sacred space
where saints have knelt and prayed.
I often feel, O God, that I want to take off my shoes
and stand on holy ground –
this is none other than a gate of heaven.

Pray without Ceasing

16 May

Jesus, our Friend and Brother,
we give thanks for our friends –
for their kindness,
for their support,
for their love.
We pray for those who don't have any friends.
May they turn to you
knowing that you are the Friend of the friendless.

17 May

May Christ surround you with his presence,
May he enfold you with his love,
May he fill you with his peace,
And when we are absent one from another,
May he watch over you
And keep you in his care.

18 May

God of the saints, we give thanks
for those who have nurtured us,
touched our lives with their spirituality,
those who have inspired us,
those who have encouraged us.
May we walk in their footsteps
till our journey's end.

19 May

God of wisdom and might,
All power and majesty are yours,
We give thanks for our creation,
For our redemption,
For all the gifts you give us abundantly,
We worship you and praise your holy name.

20 May

Lord Jesus, you called your disciples
to leave everything and follow you.
You call us to follow –
perhaps to turn our backs on home and family,
to leave the land of our birth,
to suffer financial or physical hardship –
maybe even death.
May we be willing to take up our cross daily
and follow you.

21 May

Prepare our hearts, O Saviour, that at your Second Coming,
we may be found ready and eager to greet you
when you come in glory.
Keep us ever watchful and alert.

Pray without Ceasing

22 May

O God, we bring before you our world –
full of greed and the love of money,
pleasure-seeking and self-centredness.
Touch the hearts of those involved
in financial affairs, that they may seek
to be honest and transparent in all their dealing.
May they realise that they are ultimately accountable to you.

23 May

As I pause in the stillness,
May I be conscious of your presence,
May I wait upon you, O God,
Help me just to be quiet,
To turn my mind from earthly things,
To listen to your voice –
That still, small voice.

24 May

Lord Jesus, you took the little children
in your arms and blessed them.
We pray for all children – the homeless,
the refugee, the abused, the unloved.
May the homeless find shelter,
the refugee, a secure place,
the abused, a safe haven
and the unloved, the love
every child needs and deserves.

May

25 May

God of every age, may we respect the past,
herald the future, but live the present.

26 May

Lord, you will come as a thief in the night –
suddenly with no warning,
yet you will return as King of kings
and Lord of lords and every knee
shall bow when you appear.
May I be awake and watchful,
eager to greet you when you come in glory.

27 May

Heavenly Father, I'm aging,
My body aches, I forget things,
I can't walk as fast as I once did,
I don't like what is happening to me.
Just help me to trust you,
You have a plan for me,
You brought me to birth,
You haven't finished with me yet,
O Changeless God, you know my end.

28 May

Lord, you give us many gifts.
May we seek above all to have love
that is patient and kind, not jealous or proud
not keeping a tally of past wrongs.
But love that protects and trusts and hopes.
Love that forgives and forgives and keeps on forgiving,
love that is greater than knowledge or prophecy –
a small measure of your perfect love.

Pray without Ceasing

29 May

On those who are in pain,
Come, Lord, with your healing touch,
On little children suffering,
Come, Lord, with your healing touch,
On those awaiting surgery,
Come, Lord, with your healing touch,
On those depressed or anxious,
Come, Lord, with your healing touch,
On those troubled in body or mind,
Come, Lord, with your healing touch.

30 May

Lord Jesus, you bore on your body
the wounds of human sin,
yet you entrusted your Church
to care for our broken humanity.
Draw us closer to yourself
with the bonds of love,
that we may witness to that love
in this world in all its brokenness.

31 May

For the gift of each new day, we thank you, O God,
For nights of sleep, we thank you, O God,
For the beauty of each sunrise, we thank you, O God,
For the peace that comes at sunset, we thank you, O God,
For the seasons of the year, we give thanks, O God.
For the diversity of creation, we give thanks, O God,
For all your gifts to us, we give thanks, O God.

✿ ✿ ✿ ✿ ✿ ✿ ✿

June

1 June

Help me this day, O Lord,
not to dwell on my own troubles,
but on the troubles of others.
Be with those for whom this day
will bring pain or sorrow or worry or anxiety.
May they turn to you in their need
and find that your strength is made
perfect in weakness.

2 June

We pray, dear Lord, for all those who do not know you.
For those who have never heard your gospel of love
or who have rejected you.
For people of other faiths
who do not acknowledge you as Saviour.
Open their eyes and touch their hearts
that they may see you, Lord Jesus,
as the complete revelation
of the Father's divine love.

3 June

I have much to answer for, Lord God –
Words spoken that would have been
better left unsaid,
Words that should have been spoken
but remained unformed and silent,
Deeds done that would have been
better left undone,
Deeds of kindness that remained
inert and impotent.
Forgive my sins of omission and commission
and help me to seek to follow the example
of your dear Son, Jesus Christ.

4 June

Give us unadulterated joy within, O God,
that we may shine as lights to your glory.
May people see the joy of the Lord in us
and want to have that same joy.
Help us to show people Jesus.

5 June

Lord, you are slow to anger
and show great mercy,
yet you are our Maker and our Judge.
May we live according to your will
that at the last day we might hear you say,
'Well done, good and faithful servant.'

6 June

I worry about the future, loving Father,
What will tomorrow bring?
If it is pain, help me to bear it,
If it is anxiety, may I cast my care on you,
If it is financial hardship
may I trust you for my daily needs,
If it is sorrow, may I know
that underneath me are your everlasting arms
and that you will never let me go.

7 June

Lord, you make streams in the desert –
Water to refresh, to cleanse, to purify.
Water, the outward visible sign of baptism.
Give us that Living Water
that springs up to give us
eternal life.

June

8 June

O Holy Spirit, your voice is heard
in the gentle breeze.
Your breath gives life to the world.
Fill us with a sense of wonder and awe
that we may see beauty in each sunset,
in the intricate pattern of veins on each leaf,
in every living thing.

9 June

There is so much to give thanks for, O God.
Help me to persevere, without grumbling,
without complaining, without self-pity.
May I run the race of life that is set before me
with my eyes fixed on Jesus.

10 June

Whether we are on the mountain top of joy
or in the valley of despair, O God,
you are always present.
You sustain us, you strengthen us, you love us.
You are our help in every kind of trouble.
You share with us in our gladness
and feel for us in our sadness.

11 June

Lord of light, you came to this world
once as a tiny Baby.
When you come again it will be in majesty and glory
as King of kings and Lord of lords.
May we be found watching and waiting,
ready to welcome you.

Pray without Ceasing

12 June

I'm frustrated, Lord, there are too many things
happening at once.
I just want to escape to somewhere quiet
and find some peace,
away from the maddening crowd.
May your peace wash over me
and envelope me.

13 June

Jesus, Good Shepherd, guide us,
Jesus, Bread of Life, nourish us,
Jesus, the True Vine, strengthen us,
Jesus, the Resurrection and the Life, raise us,
Jesus, Emmanuel, God with us,
Jesus, the Way, the Truth and the Life, receive us.

14 June

God of every age, we give thanks
for all those who have nurtured us,
guided and inspired us.
Those who have shown us Jesus
by their own examples.
May we too seek to nurture,
guide and inspire others.

15 June

Thank you, Lord, for the gift of music –
to soothe,
to motivate,
to inspire,
to transport us to the very gates of heaven,
to bring back memories – both joyous and poignant.
May our lives be a symphony of praise.

16 June

Lord God, change our apathy into action,
Our greed into generosity,
Our coldness into compassion,
Our hate into love,
Our judgement into acceptance,
Our pride into humility.
Make us your new creation.

17 June

God of the morning,
you give us a new day –
with all its potential,
its problems,
its possibilities.
God of the noon day,
you give us encouragement
and energy and enthusiasm.
God of the evening,
you give us relaxation
and rest and refreshment.
May we use each hour to your glory.

18 June

Loving Saviour, you draw us to yourself
with the cords of love,
you carry us on your shoulders
through the rough places,
you surround us with your presence,
you guide us when the way
before us is unknown,
and you will never forsake us.

19 June

Thank you, Lord, for colours,
The vibrant spectrum of the rainbow,
The palest shades to deepest gold
of each sunrise and sunset,
The emerald green of the fields,
The rich brown of the soil,
The cobalt blue of the sky,
The diversity of colour of each flower,
The deepest blue of the oceans.
You, the Master Artist used your palette
to create such beauty.

20 June

Good and gracious God,
In your holy Word,
May I hear you,
In the beauty of nature,
May I see you,
In a loving touch,
May I feel your presence.

21 June

Lord, may I see your face
in other people's faces,
that I may find your presence
in everyone I meet.

22 June

With your love, enfold us,
With your protection, keep us,
With your presence, surround us
And with your Spirit, fill us,
Lord God, each day, each night.

23 June

Holy Spirit, Comforting One,
Blow over this earth:
Where countries are greedy and affluent,
May they learn to share;
Where countries are ravaged by war,
May peace come;
Where countries are stricken by famine,
May their needs be provided;
Where countries are proud and arrogant,
May they seek humility.
May your kingdom come
and may the earth be filled
with the glory of God
as the waters cover the sea.

24 June

Saviour, with your heart so tender,
Come to those who grieve this day,
Those who mourn the loss of loved ones,
Be with them, O Lord, we pray.
And for those who suffer illness,
Come with healing, touch this day,
Those who sit and wait in anguish,
Be with them, O Lord, we pray.
Man of Sorrows, loving Saviour,
Come with peace to those this day,
All who grieve and fear and worry,
Be with them, O Lord, we pray.

25 June

Merciful God, look with pity on us
your frail creatures.
Remember that we are but dust.
Forgive us our sins and grant us
grace to amend our lives.

26 June

Holy Spirit, come upon us.
Guide, strengthen, protect and fill us.
Renew us and the whole of creation.
Come upon us
with the power of Pentecost.

27 June

God of harmony,
My body is tense
My mind is in a whirl.
Help me to relax in your presence,
Give me patience to wait, to be still.
May your peace flow over me
and through me,
Calm my frenzied mind
and my tired body, I pray.

28 June

Risen Lord, come,
Raise the down-hearted,
Strengthen the weak,
Comfort the bereaved,
Give peace to those who are anxious,
Risen Lord, come, bring healing and wholeness
to a wounded world.

29 June

Lord, be with me
when the future is bleak,
when I feel old or sick,
when I am full of fears,
when I even doubt my own faith.
My Lord, stand by me
and with me, I pray.

30 June

Living Lord, may your radiance
shine upon my path,
may your strength
lift the heaviness of my heart,
may your guiding hand
lead me in your way,
and finally, at journey's end,
may you receive my soul.

1 July

God of beauty,
you paint the colours of the rainbow
with your divine palette.
The rainbow – your promise
that you will never again destroy
the earth by water.
When we see a rainbow in the sky
may we remember your pledge
to humankind and be thankful.

2 July

God of mercy,
Give us wisdom to understand you,
Determination to seek you,
Patience to allow you to act,
Eyes to see you,
A heart to dwell upon you,
And a life to proclaim your message.
(Inspired by a prayer by St Benedict)

July

3 July

I thank you, loving Father
for the assurance that I am your child,
you love me and care for me.
You are always with me,
you call me by my name
and I know that I am yours.
You raise me up and carry me
on eagles' wings.

4 July

Good and gracious God,
We give thanks for everything
that is beautiful – the sparkling sea,
the stars at night, the rippling river,
the snow-capped mountains,
the diversity of all animal and plant life.
All have been fashioned by your creative hands
and you have committed
all things to our care.
May we be faithful stewards
of all that you entrust to us.

5 July

God of power and might,
we bring before you
all places ravaged by war.
We pray for those who have lost
loved ones, homes or livelihoods in conflict.
Look with compassion on those
who are maimed or injured
as a result of warfare.
We long for the day when your Son
will come again to reign in glory.

6 July

Lord Jesus, when everything around us
is changing, you remain the same –
yesterday, today and forever.
We thank you for this assurance.
You have told us that you will be with us
till the end of the world.
May we grasp the truth of that promise.

7 July

Most merciful Redeemer,
we pray for all those suffering pain,
particularly those who are near and dear to us.
Let the hem of your garment touch them
and stretch out your healing hand
upon them and make them well.

8 July

With joy, Lord, fill us,
With light, Lord, guide us,
With peace, Lord, quieten us,
With love, Lord, stir us,
With your Spirit, Lord, empower us,
to live, to think, to speak for you.

9 July

Lord, you are the vine,
we are the branches.
Help us to draw strength from you
and not to try to cope on our own,
for without you we can do nothing that will last.

10 July

Look with love, Lord God,
On your creation,
Blighted by human sin,
Yet redeemed with the blood of Christ.
We give thanks for his sacrifice –
Once, only once and for all humanity.
May we be drawn
with the cords of love
that we might show people Jesus
by our lives.

11 July

You give me strength to work, O God,
You shine light on my path,
You give me peace of mind,
You endow me with the power I need,
Help me to walk with you every day
of my earthly pilgrimage.

12 July

Merciful God, you tenderly gather
your children to yourself,
as a mother hen protects her chicks.
We thank you for your care
and your patience when we stray
from the right path.
Thank you that we can cry 'Abba, Father'
and know that you love us.
May we respond to that love
by seeking to live for you alone
rather than for our own selfish whims.

13 July

We praise you, Creator God,
for the animals that share our lives –
for our dogs and cats and other pets.
We give thanks for their loyalty and love,
for their understanding of our moods,
for their patience.
We remember those who have walked
the road of life, with its joys and sorrows
but are no longer here with us,
but are safe in your care.

14 July

Lord, it only takes a spark to get a fire going,
kindle a flame of love
within my cold heart,
a flame that spreads to friend and foe alike,
to neighbour, to family near and far,
that all may be warmed
by the glow of your presence
and the transforming power
of your Holy Spirit.

15 July

Almighty God, you have the power
to help and to heal.
We uphold before you any we know
who are in any kind of need –
our friends, our neighbours and ourselves.
May we find that your grace is sufficient
whatever the need.

16 July

Come softly to us, O Lord,
when we are in grief and despair.
You are the Man of Sorrows,
well acquainted with our heartache.
Draw near to us
and keep us in your mighty power.
You promised that those who mourn
would be comforted.
May we claim the reality of that truth
for our own.

17 July

Bounteous God, you give us
Strength to serve you,
Grace to love you,
Obedience to follow you,
Joy to praise you
and a life to glorify you.

18 July

Lord Jesus, you came that we might have
life in all its fullness – its abundance.
May we live life to the full
and for your glory.
Help us to greet each day
as an opportunity to serve you.

Pray without Ceasing

19 July

God of eternity, one day I shall die,
I have no idea of when or where or how.
I thank you that such knowledge is hidden from me.
May I be prepared to meet you
at journey's end.

20 July

Help us, O God of peace,
To cherish moments of quiet reflection,
When we can be still and meditate,
When we can be alone with you,
When we can remove other thoughts,
And wait upon you in silent contemplation.

21 July

Lord, we pray for all those broken
in body, mind or spirit,
Those in broken relationships,
Those with broken hearts,
Lift them up, O God,
For you alone can make us whole.

22 July

God of the whole human race,
We pray for the nations of the world,
May tolerance replace bigotry,
May there be peace instead of war,
May sufficiency replace hunger,
May generosity come in place of greed,
And may love, the greatest gift,
Overcome hate.

23 July

Wherever we go, you Lord
are there with us,
Whatever we experience, you Lord
are there with us,
Whatever road we travel, you Lord
are there with us,
Whatever we feel, you Lord
are there with us.

24 July

May the light of God
shine upon you,
may the love of God
shine out from you,
and may the blessing of God,
Father, Son and Holy Spirit
fill you with the light of Christ.

25 July

Lord, you come to us
in bread and wine
to strengthen us and to nourish us,
Lord, you speak to us
in your holy Word
to enlighten and encourage us.
May we be aware of your presence
and be ever alert as you speak to us
in word and sacrament.

26 July

God of beauty, you paint the sky
with a myriad of shades at sunrise and sunset.
You are lavish in your bounty to us.
May we appreciate your creation,
help us to cherish it and protect it.

27 July

Thank you for music, O Lord,
music to challenge, music to console,
music to inspire, music to glorify.
May the music of earth
be united with the symphony of heaven
when you come in glory.

28 July

Eternal God, we give thanks for those we have loved
and are now at rest with you,
We still miss them, their loving greeting,
their tender touch.
Draw near to us, O God,
when we feel alone and bereft.
Comfort us and support us
through the dark moments of our lives.

29 July

Lord, you give us hope,
You give us love,
You give us yourself in bread and wine,
To strengthen and nourish us,
May we feed on you in our hearts
by faith with thanksgiving.

30 July

May your holy angels protect us,
May your saints and martyrs inspire us,
May wise mentors encourage us,
And may the Father, Son and Holy Spirit,
bless, guide and sanctify us.

31 July

Thank you, Lord Jesus,
For those Epiphany moments when you reveal
yourself to us in some special way.
Open our eyes, that we may see,
Open our ears, that we may hear,
Open our hearts, that we may love,
May we be inspired by those special moments
of revelation.

1 August

Loving Saviour, fill our minds
with all that is good and pure and holy.
There is so much evil in the world.
May we shine as lights in the darkness
that our lives may show people Jesus.

2 August

Lord, in our journeying, protect us,
In our doings, guide us,
In our sleeping, refresh us,
In our waking, motivate us,
In our speaking, direct us,
In our dying, receive us.

Pray without Ceasing

3 August

We pray for Christian unity.
From pride and bigotry,
Good Lord, deliver us,
From feeling we are right,
Good Lord, deliver us,
From intolerance and deep-seated prejudices,
Good Lord, deliver us.
Help us to celebrate our common ground
rather than accentuating our differences.

4 August

Lord, you have said blessed are those
who are persecuted falsely for your sake.
This is a hard saying to accept.
Give me the grace I need
to bear my own trials and tribulations.

5 August

Almighty God, your Word will remain forever.
Life is eternal and love is immortal.
May we realise how quickly this world
will pass away, and pursue those things
that are good and everlasting.

August

6 August

Only a great person can be humble,
and it is that humility which makes the person great.
Blessed Lord, you left the courts of heaven
to come to earth and be born as a helpless baby,
you were baptised yet you had not sinned,
you walked the dusty roads of Palestine
and knelt to wash your disciples' feet.
You died a criminal's death on the Cross
and rose again to give us eternal life.
You, the Lord of Heaven, humbled yourself
to take the servant role.
Give us a measure of that humility, we pray.

7 August

Lord, your heart is filled with love
for your Creation.
You walk the way of the world's wounded.
You share our joys and our crushing sorrows.
You bind up the broken-hearted.
You love us and care for us.
Thank you for this assurance.

8 August

Lord Jesus, you are our Friend and Brother,
Our Saviour and our Guide.
Help us to serve you with joy, with love,
and faithful obedience till our lives' end.

9 August

The cutting remark, Father forgive,
The withering glare, Father forgive,
The way we treat others, Father forgive,
The way others treat us, Father forgive.
Lord, your heart must break
because of our words and actions.
Forgive us and change us.

10 August

Lord, you admonish us not to set
our hearts on earthly treasures,
yet you know we need money to live.
We pray for those in financial difficulty –
through loss of job or illness
or as a result of their own foolishness,
for those facing the loss of their home.
May they seek wise advice
from those willing to help them.
May they turn to you in their distress
and hear you say 'Come to me all
who are weary and burdened with life
and I will give you rest.'

11 August

Jesus, Son of the living God,
You calmed the storm to reassure
your frightened disciples.
So often our lives are fraught with storms,
Surround us with your protection
and breathe peace into our souls.

12 August

Welcoming Lord, your arms are always
stretched out to enfold us.
Help us to show your welcoming love
to each other,
whatever our race or creed.
Fill us, O Welcoming Christ,
with your all-embracing love.

13 August

May our hearts be little hermitages, O God,
where we can draw aside
from the busyness of life
and come before you in silence,
Help us to wait upon you
in quietness and adoration
and allow your peace
to encircle us and flow through us.

14 August

Creator God, we give thanks for dogs –
for their love and companionship,
for mountain rescue dogs which find
injured people in the snow,
for guide dogs and hearing dogs
which improve the quality of life
for blind and deaf people,
for 'sniffer' dogs which seek to keep us safe.
And most of all, for our beloved pets –
past and present – which give us
such unstinting love and devotion
and share our joys and our heartaches.

15 August

Lord Jesus, you are the Good Shepherd,
look with love on your wayward, wandering sheep.
Guide us back to the narrow way
that leads to life.
Keep us from falling into rough places
and save us from turning away from you.
When we hear your tender voice calling us,
may we respond and return
to the safety of your fold.

16 August

Gracious God, help me to be more aware
of people's feelings.
Guard my tongue in what I say,
open my ears to the cry of the needy.
Fill my heart with even a small measure of your love.
May I be Christ to others.

17 August

God of the human race,
may prejudice find no place in our society.
Help us to accept others as they are,
not as we want them to be.
May we welcome and be open
to the stranger, the refugee,
for you have made each in your own image.

August

18 August

At the end of each day, help us to admit
where we have failed, loving Father,
give us the grace to begin again
with your gift of each new day.

19 August

God of the oceans deep,
we pray for all those who risk their lives at sea.
The fishermen who must earn their living
in all weathers.
The lifeboat crews who brave the elements
to save others.
The helicopter pilots who use difficult manoeuvres
to rescue those in need of assistance.
Your Son whispered 'Peace, be still'
to calm the storm.
Be with those who put their own lives at risk
in order to rescue those in peril on the seas.

20 August

Lord Jesus, you withdrew to quiet places
to spend time alone with your Father.
You saw the wildflowers in the fields
and the birds in the air
and knew that he cared for each one.
May we make time in our busy lives
to just be still and know that you are God.
Help us to 'take time out' to appreciate
the beauty and diversity of your creation.

Pray without Ceasing

21 August

God of our pilgrimage,
May we journey in faith and love,
Rejoicing and eager to serve you.
Grant us a glimpse of your glory,
As we seek to follow you –
The Way, the Truth and the Life.

22 August

Use my hands, Lord,
To reach out to others,
Use my feet, Lord,
To walk in your way,
Use my eyes, Lord,
To see the beauty of creation,
Use my ears, Lord,
To hear your message,
Use my mouth, Lord,
To praise your name,
Use my heart, Lord,
To spread your love,
Use me, body, mind and spirit,
To glorify you.

23 August

From hardness of heart, Lord, be keeping us,
From deliberate sin, Lord, be saving us,
From unclean thoughts, Lord, be sparing us,
From thoughtless deeds, Lord, be preserving us,
From unkind words, Lord, be keeping us.

24 August

God of grace and mercy,
today I'm miserable and it's my own fault,
I can't blame anyone else.
Forgive me, and give me the
strength and determination
to do better and not to fail you.

25 August

O God, you would enfold
earth and heaven in one single peace.
Help us to realise the futility of anger and wars.
Give peace to your Church,
peace among nations,
peace in our homes
and peace in our hearts.

26 August

Lord, when we stray from your path,
we are skating on thin ice.
Save us from falling,
save us from ourselves,
and raise us up to be the people
you want us to be.

27 August

Almighty God, may we be willing
to lay our lives on the altar
as a living sacrifice to you.
May we submit our hearts,
minds and wills to your gentle rule.
May we surrender everything we are or ever hope to be,
to you, our God.

28 August

Welcoming God, help us
to be friendly and open with others.
May they not feel excluded from our midst
because of race, religion or background.
May we see Christ in every being
and love as he loves us.

29 August

Lord of light, as the sunshine
warms our bodies and lifts our spirits,
so may our hearts be open
to your life-giving power.
Inflame our cold hearts
that we may shine as lights in the world
so that others may feel drawn
to the warmth of your love.

30 August

Creator God, each new day is a gift from you,
A new chapter in our lives,
It comes with problems and challenges,
With sorrow and joy.
May we accept each day, whatever it brings,
Knowing that you are there with us,
Whatever the future holds.

31 August

God of gentleness, yet God of judgement,
look in love upon your frail creatures.
Forgive our shortcomings,
our yielding to temptation,
our many sins – of deeds done and not done.
Fill us with the power of your Spirit
that we may walk in the newness of life
and in your strength.

1 September

God of love, we give thanks for those
who love us in spite of our failings.
Help us to respond to that love
by never taking them for granted.
Bless them and keep them in your care.

2 September

May your peace flow through us
and from us, O Lord,
peace to those we love,
peace to those we meet,
peace to those we find hard to like,
peace to our neighbours,
peace to our friends,
peace to our world,
and let it begin with me.

3 September

God of creativity,
You fashion each snowflake
from a myriad of unique crystals.
You blanket the earth in a mantle
of purest white snow.
We thank you that although our sins are as scarlet
they shall be white as the driven snow.

4 September

Thank you, risen Lord,
that because of your death on the cross,
we now live under grace not the old law.
You came that we might have life in all its fullness,
all its abundance,
from the storehouse of your bounty,
good measure, pressed down
and overflowing.
Help us to live in the freedom
you have given us.

5 September

Give us obedience to follow you, O Lord,
Give us willingness to serve you,
Give us perseverance to endure,
Give us joy to praise you,
And a lifelong commitment
to walk in your way.

6 September

Lord Jesus, you were baptised
though you had not sinned.
We pray for all those recently baptised –
for tiny babies brought by their parents
or relatives, for those who are older
and have made the choice for themselves.
Bless each one as they seek to remain true
to their baptismal promises.
Strengthen those from other faiths
who have been baptised Christians
and now face alienation from their families
and communities.
May the power of your Spirit
descend on each one and affirm their faith.

7 September

God of all wisdom,
take my mind, take my intellect,
take the knowledge I have,
and use them to your glory,
and when I am forgetful,
give me patience with myself,
and help me to entrust
my future to your care.

8 September

O God, help me to serve you better,
help me to love you more,
help me to follow you always,
help me to surrender my whole self –
body, mind and spirit –
to be used in your service.

Pray without Ceasing

9 September

When I come into your presence, Lord,
I feel the warmth of your love enfolding me,
your welcoming arms embracing me.
May I feel secure in the knowledge
that you have called me by name
and I am yours.

10 September

Creator God, we pray for all animals
that are mistreated.
Those that are forced to carry heavy loads
more than they can bear,
those beaten by cruel, often ignorant, owners,
those denied any veterinary care,
those abandoned without food or water or any shelter.
Look in love and compassion
on your suffering creatures
that they may find some kindness
in the midst of their trials.

11 September

Mighty God, our refuge and our strength,
be with us in times of trouble.
Help us to have that assurance that nothing,
not even death, can separate us from you,
for you will never leave us nor forsake us.

12 September

God of the harvest,
bless those who labour on the land,
be with them through drought, flood and pestilence.
Help us to be mindful of the effort involved
in providing our food
and may we ever acknowledge
your hand in providing for us.

13 September

Loving God, we pray for young people
whose lives hold so much potential
and so many possibilities.
Give them strength to resist temptation
in whatever form it comes.
Save them from turning to drugs
and excessive use of alcohol
and so ruining their lives
and the lives of those who love them.
Give us a listening ear
and a caring spirit that we may encourage
them to follow you.

14 September

Lord, help me to follow you,
help me to serve you,
help me to obey you,
help me to honour you,
help me to love you,
and finally, at the end
of my earthly pilgrimage,
may I hear you say
'Well done, good and faithful servant.'

15 September

Almighty God, we pray
for all Christian rulers
that by the example of their lives,
they may exercise their authority
in ways pleasing to you
and for the good of all peoples.

16 September

Forgive my pride, Lord Jesus,
and my sense of self-importance.
When I want to be noticed,
and made to feel important,
may I remember how you knelt
to wash your disciples' feet.
Give me a sense of humility
and may I be willing to serve.

17 September

God of time and space,
a day is as a thousand years,
a millisecond as a century to you.
Creator of everything,
may we use our short time
on the world's stage wisely,
and in eternity
may we praise you forever.

18 September

Lord, our Saviour and our Redeemer,
you were born of the blessed virgin.
Guide and help all mothers
that they may love and nurture their children.
May they regard them as sacred gifts from you,
and seek to lead them in your way.

19 September

Generous God, you teach us
that it is more blessed to give
than to receive.
Help us from the bounty
you lavish on us,
to open our hearts to the poor, the needy,
the homeless, the dispossessed.
May we see you in every living being
and acknowledge that we are all
made in your image.

20 September

Defend, O Lord, your servant,
that strengthened by your grace
I may continue to be yours forever.
Endow me daily with your Spirit
until I come to your everlasting kingdom.

21 September

Holy and strong God, be with those
persecuted for their faith.
Give them strength to endure
despite the taunts of family and friends.
In the face of physical violence and even death,
may they stand firm in the knowledge
that you will never desert them.

22 September

Lord, in life, direct us,
in trouble, calm us,
in danger, protect us,
in sickness, succour us,
in sorrow, comfort us,
and in death, receive us.

23 September

God of resurrection,
thank you for the springtime –
the beginning of new life,
for bulbs sprouting,
for newborn lambs skipping around their mothers,
for warmer, longer days,
for hope after a long winter.
Breathe new life into our weary souls
and raise us to new heights
of joy and service.

24 September

Good and gracious God,
be with those who are facing
momentous decisions that will affect
the rest of their lives.
Whether it be a different job,
choice of a partner for life,
a move to another country,
a sudden illness
or financial hardship,
may they turn to you
for guidance and support.

25 September

You offer me your yoke which is easy
and your burden which is light, dear Saviour.
I am weary, I feel drained, I need to hear
your soothing voice of invitation,
'Come to me all who are heavy laden
and I will give you rest.'
May I respond to your loving arms
stretched out to me in welcome
and may I experience
the reality of your promise.

26 September

God of all knowledge,
may we open your Word more often,
may we read it and obey it,
may we feed on it
and be receptive to its message.
Your Word is a lamp to direct our feet
and a light to show us the right path.

Pray without Ceasing

27 September

Lord, you are the Great Physician.
Look with your tender compassion
on all who suffer pain.
Be with them
through the long sleepless hours.
May they find that your strength
is made perfect in their weakness.
Let the hem of your healing robe
touch them and bring wholeness.

28 September

God of hospitality, we pray
for neighbours near and far,
for friends old and new,
for those we love dearly
and those whom we find hard to bear,
as well as those who find us difficult.
Give us patience with each other
and expansive hearts
to accept rather than condemn.

29 September

Creator God, we pray
for all animal lovers
especially those mourning
the loss of a beloved pet.
As we look back over the years
we remember those who have shared our lives –
our joys and our sorrows,
our hopes and our disappointments.
We give thanks for their undemanding love
and their constant devotion.
Keep them safe in your loving care, dear Father.

30 September

Lord Jesus, I have been deeply hurt
by one I considered a friend
and for no good reason.
You too have been hurt
and betrayed by a friend.
I thank you that you
will never turn against me.

1 October

Christ of the manger,
grant us humility.
Christ of the mountain top,
show us a glimpse of your glory.
Christ of the Cross,
stir our cold hearts to respond to your love.
Christ of the empty tomb,
grant us eternal life.

2 October

Wash me, holy God,
and cleanse me from my sin –
both deliberate and unintentional.
Give me the will to persevere
in following you.
Wash me whiter than snow
and make me pure within.
Forgive the past,
help me to amend the present
and bless the future, that I may live
according to your will.

3 October

Quietly you come to us
in bread and wine, O Lord.
There is no fanfare,
just an abiding peace
that you feed us and nourish us.
Strengthen us with the bread of life
and the cup of salvation.
You will continue to walk with us day by day,
and indeed till our journey's end.

4 October

God our Creator and Redeemer,
you have made this world beautiful – so diverse, yet so fragile.
May we be faithful stewards of all that you have entrusted to us.
Help us to protect and conserve, not pollute and destroy.
May we care for all animal and plant life.
You have made the universe for us to delight in.
May we guard against its exploitation,
and share its bounty fairly and justly with all.

5 October

Lord Jesus, you carry the lambs in your arms,
look with your pity on those who have lost a child.
Comfort them and support them,
may they know that you are the Man of Sorrows
well acquainted with their grief.
In their anger and disappointment,
in their shattered dreams and recriminations,
console them, dear Lord.

6 October

Perhaps, if I was walking
in someone else's shoes,
I would not be so judgemental, Lord,
I would not be so impatient,
I would not be so ready to condemn.
Help me to be more accepting,
more forgiving,
more like you, my Lord.

7 October

Lord of light and love,
shine into our dark lives
that we may reflect your glory.
Come into the hidden recesses of our lives
where long-held grudges and prejudices dwell.
Lighten our lives with the radiance
of your presence that we may be
children of the Light.

8 October

Gracious God,
give me patience to listen, to wait,
give me quietness to meditate, to think,
give me love to share, to care,
give me motivation to act, to do,
give me peace to be calm, to refresh.

Pray without Ceasing

9 October

God of all wisdom,
we pray for all places of learning.
Give to tutors and teachers
a real desire to inspire their students.
May those who learn be keen
to listen and absorb what they are taught.
Help them to be grateful
for the privilege of gaining knowledge,
and may they ever be mindful
that you are the source of all knowledge.

10 October

Lord, when I am tired, refresh me,
When I am cast down, lift me up,
When I am anxious, calm me,
When I am frustrated, encourage me,
When I am lonely, befriend me,
When I am frightened, encircle me,
When I am grieving, comfort me.

11 October

My Lord and my God,
I fail you so often, forgive me
and strengthen my resolve to serve you.
The world presses in on me
and my own stubborn will takes control.
Touch my heart with your love
and fill me with your Spirit
that I may surrender my will to you.

October

12 October

God of new life, give us springtime in our lives –
new hopes, new dreams, new possibilities.
As bulbs sprout from something brown and dead
into beautiful flowers, so may we blossom
into the kind of person you want us to be.

13 October

Lord,
in the time of trial, strengthen us,
In the time of danger, protect us,
In the time of doubt, assure us,
In the time of sickness, heal us,
In the time of exhaustion, refresh us,
In the time of grief, comfort us,
And all for your love's sake.

14 October

God of the universe,
You set the stars in place,
You formed the oceans and the dry land,
You made the tiniest insect and the mightiest whale,
You created the sun and the moon,
You fashioned man, and woman to be his helper,
Yet you care for me.

15 October

Give me compassion, gracious Lord,
fill my heart with your love,
fill my life with your power,
fill my mind with your peace,
and fill me, use me to your glory
that I may show your love to all I meet.

16 October

God our Father, guide and direct
all who are fathers,
may they realise their responsibility
to love and nurture their children
as you love us all.
And for those abused by their fathers,
may they cast themselves
with all their anger and anxiety
into your loving arms.
Help them to find that place of peace
near to your loving heart.

17 October

Lord Jesus, I would lay my weary head
on your shoulder,
I am tired, oh so tired.
Come to me, Lord, in your renewing power
and lift me up.
Help me to soar on eagles' wings.
May I run and not be weary.
May I walk and not faint.

18 October

O God, cleanse me and quieten me,
fill me and mould me
that I may always seek to do
your holy will in whatever
I think or say or do.

19 October

Lord, we regret our wrong doings,
we repent of all that would grieve your heart,
we rejoice in your bounty,
we remember true pleasures with gratitude,
we recall memories of happy days.
Lead us and guide us through the storms of life.

20 October

Help us, living Lord,
to grow in holiness and in love
that we might be the people you would have us be.
May we reveal your glory in our lives.

21 October

Son of God, yet born of Mary,
bless those who are mothers.
May they realise the privilege that is theirs –
to hold a baby in their arms.
Help them to love and nurture
their children and may they encourage
them to serve you all their lives.

22 October

High King of Heaven,
you gave us voices to praise you
and the ability to play musical instruments.
We pray for all musicians, for composers,
for performers, for choirs and soloists,
particularly those who use their talents
to bring glory to your name.
We look to the day when the music
of earth will be joined with the heavenly symphony.

23 October

Help me, Lord God, to worship you
in the beauty of holiness.
May I enter your courts
with praise and thanksgiving.
May I be still and know
that you are with me.
May my prayers rise to heaven
like fragrant incense.
May I leave your sanctuary
secure in the knowledge
that you are with me.

24 October

Holy God, may we see all people in this global village
as our sisters and brothers.
Be with those who live in fear of their lives
through war or religious persecution.
Walk beside those who suffer
violence and torture.
Let there be peace on earth
and may I, for my part,
do all I can to make this happen.

25 October

From greed, Lord, be keeping us,
From anger, Lord be saving us,
From pride, Lord, be sparing us,
From self-will, Lord be directing us,
From love of money, Lord, be freeing us.

26 October

God of wisdom and grace,
I need to change.
Open my cold heart to the power
of your Holy Spirit.
Help me to show the fruits
of love, joy and peace,
of gentleness and patience
in my life.

27 October

God of the sunset, God of the dawn,
God of the rainbow, God of the storm,
God of each flower, God of the sky,
God of the ocean, and mountain high.

28 October

Eternal Father, we come before you in penitence,
forgive our sins.
We have failed you
so many times and missed the mark.
Give us grace to amend our lives
and may we seek to follow you more faithfully.

29 October

Lord Jesus, you walked on water
and calmed the storm.
We think of all those whose lives
are bound up with the sea.
For fishermen earning their livelihood,
for coastguard staff protecting our coasts,
for lifeboat crews risking their own lives
to rescue those in difficulties,
for helicopter pilots involved
in dangerous manoeuvres,

for ships' captains guiding their vessels
through often treacherous waters.
Lord, steer my tiny craft on the sea of life
with all its troughs and crests.
Grant us safe anchorage
in the heavenly harbour.

30 October

Lord, encircle us when danger is near,
Surround us when temptations come,
Direct us when we cannot see the way ahead,
Protect us when the Devil strikes,
Save us by your Cross and Passion.

31 October

God of love and mercy, look on us
your frail creatures.
Remember that we are but dust
and to dust we shall return.
Strengthen us by the power
of your Spirit that we may live
in newness of life to your glory.

1 November

For all who died in the faith of Christ, we praise you,
For those near and dear to us, who nurtured us, we praise you,
For those who have laid down their lives willingly
For the sake of the gospel, we praise you,
For those who have run the race of life, we praise you,
For the 'big' saints and the 'little' saints,
Who have shaped our lives and inspired us, we give you thanks.

2 November

God of the ages, we give thanks
for all those who have finished
their earthly pilgrimage
and are now at rest in your care.
May we with them and blessed Mary
and all your saints share
in a joyful resurrection.
We praise you for the assurance
that you are without beginning and without end,
and that you are with us always.

3 November

Water is precious to cleanse, to purify,
You walked on it, dear Lord,
And turned water into wine at the wedding feast.
May we value it in raindrops, in rivers and in our taps,
Help us to conserve it and not waste it.
Refresh us, Lord of Living Water,
And quench our thirst.

4 November

God of compassion,
look upon all those who are growing older,
the lonely, the unloved.
Surround with your love
those whose faculties are failing,
whose bodies give constant pain,
those who have no family
or are deserted by them.
From the cradle to the grave
you care for us,
for this we give thanks.

5 November

Lord God, you created all life,
you redeemed it,
you sustain it,
you sanctify it.
May we realise
the sacred trust that is ours
as we seek to protect
and not exploit your creation.

6 November

Come, Holy Spirit,
renew the whole creation,
fill us with your power.
Breathe new life into the Church,
so often apathetic and insular,
yet you have chosen to use it
as your instrument on earth.
May every Christian seek to live
to show people Jesus.

7 November

Peace instead of war,
Health instead of disease,
Love instead of hate,
Sufficiency instead of hunger,
Generosity instead of greed,
Openness instead of intrigue,
Truth instead of lies.
Lord, we look for the day
when all things will be made
perfect and complete.
May your kingdom come.

8 November

Lord, you give us life,
You give us love,
You give us yourself –
In bread and wine.
Strengthen us, we pray,
And nourish us
with the Bread of Heaven
and the Cup of Salvation.

9 November

We give thanks, dear Lord,
For those who touch our lives
with gentleness,
with compassion,
with love,
with joy.
They light our lives like sunbeams
and the warmth of your sunshine
brings us blessing.
May I be a sunbeam to someone today.

10 November

God of love, you judge us
with infinite compassion and mercy.
We pray for all those
who grieve the loss of loved ones.
Turn the darkness of death
into the dawn of new life.
May they know that they will be reunited
in the joy of heaven.

11 November

We think today of those, O God,
who lie buried in some foreign soil
far from their native land.
We are mindful of those
who still grieve their loss
and those who suffer from war injuries.
Lord, we pray for peace
in this troubled world,
peace between nations
peace between neighbours,
peace in our hearts
and peace in our homes.

12 November

Help me to walk slower
and to sniff the flowers.
The world rushes on at a frenetic pace.
Slow me down, Lord,
and help me to be still.
May I savour each moment
and really see the beauty of creation.
Give me your peace and a willingness
to just be still.

13 November

Lord of the crystal waters,
help us to shine like diamonds.
Lord of the deep blue sky,
help us to be open to your Spirit.
Lord of the lush green hills,
nurture us with a shepherd's care.
Lord of the pebbled seashore,
give us the strength to walk the pilgrim way.
Lord of every wonder of creation,
renew us by your almighty power.

14 November

I feel I'm trying to deal with ten things at once.
Unclutter my brain, O Lord, of the trivialities of life.
Help me not to get so stirred up over little details.
May I get my priorities right – to care about the things
that really matter and not be side-tracked
by unimportant issues.
Bring order to my life and breathe peace into my soul.

15 November

Merciful God, look with compassion on your people.
Strengthen those suffering hardship.
Encourage those whose faith is wavering.
Guide those who are testing their vocation.
Uphold those who are persecuted
for their Christian belief.

Pray without Ceasing

16 November

By your Cross and Passion, Lord, you save us.
By your Death and Resurrection, you raise us
and give us the promise of life eternal.
May we deny ourselves daily
and take up our cross and follow you.

17 November

Lord, help me to recognise
that I am answerable to you for my sins.
May I not point the finger
too readily at others.
Focus my mind on the beam
that is in my own eye,
and not the speck
that is in my brother's eye.

18 November

God of love,
open our eyes to your creation,
open our ears to your call,
open our minds to your way,
open our hearts to your compassion,
open our lives to your Spirit.

19 November

Compassionate God, as we age
and our bodies ache and our eyes grow dim,
strengthen us and encourage us.
Help us to be assured
that you have called us by name
and we are yours.
Nothing can snatch us out of your hand.

20 November

Lord, you are the same
yesterday, today and forever.
You challenge us to leave
our sinful ways behind us,
to walk in newness of life.
Give us the power of your Spirit
to change us, our lives, our attitudes.

21 November

Lord Jesus, you died for me.
You died for the world –
but you died for me …
Amazing love, that you, the sinless One
should sacrifice your life
to save fallen humanity.
May we respond to that love
and seek to live to your glory.

22 November

Merciful God, you carry us on eagles' wings
and bear us on your heart when we are in grief and sorrow.
You too have known the pain of human suffering.
You comfort us as the One who laid down
your life for the sheep.

23 November

How fragile life is – easily snuffed out
like a candle in the wind – fleeting,
its end unknowable.
Help us to value our lives
and use our time wisely –
in your service, dear Lord.

24 November

God in my waking,
God in my sleeping,
God in my rising,
God in my resting,
God in my walking,
God in my sitting,
God in my living,
God in my dying.

25 November

Eternal God, our Rock and our Refuge,
protect us when the storms
and stresses of life
threaten to overcome us.
Underpin our wavering faith
with the stress-bearing girders of your love.

26 November

You put the stars in their places,
you set the planets in their orbits,
you created worlds
not yet discovered by humankind.
All beyond our imaginings,
out of the range of our knowledge.
May we proclaim you
as Creator and our Lord.

27 November

God, our Sustainer and Preserver,
we commit our broken world to you –
our own burdens we lay at your feet,
the trials of daily life.
We cast all our worries on you,
knowing that you care for us –
and for each sparrow that falls to the ground.

28 November

May we be watchful,
ever waiting for your return, Lord Jesus.
Keep us alert and ready to greet you
when you come in glory,
whatever the day or the hour.

29 November

Lord, calm my turbulent spirit,
the whirring of my mind,
the restlessness of my body.
Breathe peace into my soul,
bring quietness
into my troubled heart
and lead me with a shepherd's care.

30 November

Come to the faithful, O Lord,
Maranatha, come Lord Jesus.
To the hungry and the dispossessed,
Maranatha, come Lord Jesus.
To the persecuted and downtrodden
Maranatha, come Lord Jesus.
To the homeless and the refugee,
Maranatha, come Lord Jesus.
To the sick in mind, body or spirit,
Maranatha, come Lord Jesus.
To those who have lost everything in disasters,
Maranatha, come Lord Jesus.
To those who mourn the loss of loved ones,
Maranatha, come Lord Jesus.
To those who are dying,
Maranatha, come Lord Jesus.
When you come in great glory on the last day
may we be found watching and waiting.
Maranatha, come Lord Jesus.

1 December

Lord, you have removed our sins from us,
as far as the east is from the west
and have plunged them into the ocean depths
with a sign 'No Fishing Here'.
Assure us of your forgiveness,
and help us to forgive ourselves and each other.

2 December

High King of Heaven,
your dominions are numberless,
your power infinite,
your ways are beyond our understanding,
you are without beginning and without end,
yet you humbled yourself and came to earth
to be born as a tiny baby – vulnerable,
yet King of kings and Lord of lords.
At the end of the world,
you will return in great majesty –
and you will be acknowledged
by every person
as the High King of Heaven.

3 December

Give us grace to see you as you really are, dear Lord,
no longer the baby in the manger, helpless and dependent,
as we often want to keep you,
but rather the crucified, risen and ascended Lord
who wants our allegiance.
May we allow your kingdom to commence in our lives
that your reign of peace may come to this world
so full of fear and brokenness.

4 December

God of every nation under heaven,
you made us to be one family.
Heal our sad divisions,
break down our prejudices,
infiltrate the dark recesses
of our cold hearts and move us
to be more open to you and to each other.

5 December

Lord, you called your disciples
to leave everything and follow you
and they did.
Give us that same willingness
to follow you
in wholehearted obedience,
whatever the cost.

6 December

During this season of Advent,
prepare our hearts to celebrate
the joy of Christmas.
May we not leave you lying in the manger
but acknowledge you
as our Lord and our God.
Help us to share the good news
of your birth on earth for us
with all those in need.

7 December

Lord Jesus, help me to love you more,
to follow you with greater commitment,
to serve you in faithful surrender,
and to love you with every vestige of my being.

8 December

Most gracious God,
forgive our foolishness,
our selfishness,
our waywardness,
our sinfulness.
Help us to walk in newness of life
through the power of your Spirit.
Bless us with love, joy and peace
that we may live to your glory.

9 December

Lord, give me patience
when I want to snap.
Give me endurance
when I want to give up.
Give me assurance
when I cannot see the way ahead.
Give me guidance
when I feel I am wandering aimlessly.
Give me peace when my life is in turmoil,
but above all, give me love.

10 December

Thank you for the seasons, Almighty God,
the rich diversity of nature –
the new life and promise of resurrection
that heralds the spring,
the full glory and blossoming
of your creation in summer,
the mellowing of autumn
with its muted shades,
the beauty of winter
with the hope of another spring.

11 December

Lighten our darkness, O Lord,
by the radiance of your presence.
Fill us with joy that you were born
as a child for us.
Give us the obedience of Mary,
the humility of the shepherds,
the music of the angels,
the determination of the Wise Men,
that we may rejoice
in the Word made flesh
and follow you to our lives' end.

12 December

In the mad melee of daily life,
amidst the noise and stress,
help me to stop and be still,
even for a brief moment.
May I know that you are God.
Help me to find quietness in your presence.
May I rest in you and hear your still small voice.

13 December

God of all comfort,
we thank you for memories
of happy times shared with loved ones.
We give thanks for those who now enjoy
the fullness of eternal life.
However, we have so often failed
those we love, as they have failed us at times.
We now feel regret for things said or done,
or for words not said and deeds not done.
May we ask your forgiveness and seek to move on in faith
and newness of life.

14 December

Risen Lord, you shattered the bonds of death.
You were victorious over the grave.
Because you live, we too shall live.
We praise you that you are
the Resurrection and the Life.

15 December

Lord of the polar regions
and every coral isle,
you created a world of such diversity –
mountains and plains,
deserts and rainforests,
fjords and canyons,
rivers and oceans.
May we seek to conserve
and protect the environment
by not exploiting or polluting it,
for we are stewards of your creation.

16 December

God of life and resurrection,
be with those for whom this day
will be their last.
May they commit themselves
into your loving hands.
Be with those who wait and watch
beside them.
May they feel your comforting presence.
Be with those who seek to minister to them.
May they tend these souls
with loving care.

Pray without Ceasing

17 December

Lord of light,
you shine through our darkness,
you encourage us,
you bless us,
you surround us with your presence,
you enfold us in your love.
Be our Guide and our Shepherd wherever we go.

18 December

We give thanks, Almighty God,
for those we love and those who love us.
May we not take their love for granted.
Help us to spend quality time with them.
May we enjoy their presence
and share the good times and the bad with them.
May we support them with our prayers
and by our actions.
We thank you for the gift of love.
May we show your love
even in the smallest measure,
to all whom we meet day by day.

19 December

In this festive season,
when stress levels increase,
and tempers are often frayed,
help us to stop worrying
about sending cards and wrapping presents,
buying food and visiting friends.
May we acknowledge you
the Christ Child in the manger,
now our crucified, risen and ascended King,
as our Lord and Saviour.

20 December

In the busyness of Christmas,
Emmanuel, come to us.
As presents are wrapped and cards are written
Emmanuel, come to us.
As food is prepared and tables set,
Emmanuel, come to us.
As candles flicker and choirs sing,
Emmanuel, come to us.
As hearts are warmed by the Holy Child,
The King of kings and Lord of lords,
O come to us, abide with us,
Our Lord Emmanuel.

21 December

Holy Babe of Bethlehem,
Defend the children – of war, the abused, the unloved.
Son of God and Son of Man,
Encourage young people to dare new things for you.
Saviour of the world,
Search out the lost, the bewildered, the aimless.
Man of Galilee you walked this earth,
Journey with us on our pilgrimage.
Good Shepherd of the sheep,
Protect all animals from cruelty and exploitation.
Creator and preserver of the world,
Guard your creation against our wilful misuse.
God of wholeness, Great Physician,
Lay your healing hand on the sick.
Compassionate God, Man of Sorrows,
Come alongside the bereaved and the lonely with your presence.
Risen Lord, ascended King,
Inspire our lives with the example of your saints.
Come, Lord Jesus, come in power and glory,
and renew your whole creation.

Pray without Ceasing

22 December

Jesus, Son of Mary,
at the dawn-tide you give us life
flowing into us and you give us breath.
Jesus, Son of Mary,
at the ebb-tide you receive our last breath
flowing from us.
Receive our souls when death comes to us.

23 December

Lord, you are the Word made flesh,
you have caused new light to shine in a dark world.
Fill us with joy and peace
as we prepare to celebrate your birth.
May we rejoice in the mystery of your incarnation.
Come, Lord, be born in us today.

24 December

Almighty God, as we prepare to celebrate
the birth of your Son with rejoicing,
may we be mindful of those who mourn
the loss of loved ones at this time.
When they see an empty place at the table
comfort them, dear Lord, with your love.
Be with those who are sleeping rough
and have nowhere to call home.
We call to mind the many places
ravaged by war and civil strife and we look to the day
when peace on earth and goodwill to all
will be a reality.
We give thanks that you were willing
to send your Son to be born
of a pure virgin and to allow him to suffer
death on the Cross for our sake.

25 December

O Holy Child of Bethlehem,
our risen and ascended King,
come to us this holy day
as we ponder
the mystery of your incarnation.
May the radiance of your presence
illuminate our darkness
and bring great joy
to a wounded world.

26 December

We praise you, Lord God,
for all your saints
who have died for their faith.
Inspired by their example,
and empowered by your Spirit,
may we run with patience
the race that is set before us
looking only to Jesus,
the Author and Finisher
of our faith.

27 December

Encourage and enlighten
all those who preach and teach
your holy Word, dear Lord,
that we may seek to follow
you in the way of your truth,
that by the example of our lives
others may see Christ in us
and be drawn to serve him
till their lives' end.

Pray without Ceasing

28 December

Loving Father, we give thanks for all children
who have given their lives for their faith.
They now stand before your throne
as bright stars in your crown.
May we seek to emulate
their purity and innocence in our lives.

29 December

'The blood of the martyrs
is the seed of the church.'
We praise your name, Lord God,
for the men, women and children
in every age,
who have given their lives
for the sake of the gospel.
May we too have the courage
to stand firm in the faith of Christ
whatever the cost.

30 December

God of light and hope,
as we near the end of another year,
help us to see ourselves as we really are.
Forgive what we have been,
amend what we are
and direct what we shall be,
that we may bring glory
to your name.

31 December

God of eternity, as we stand on the threshold
of a new year, may we commit ourselves into your care,
forgive our shortcomings
and inspire us to step out bravely into the unknown,
with our hand in yours,
ready to face the future.

Prayers for Moveable Feasts

Advent

God of the Advent promise,
you sent your Son to earth
as a helpless babe,
dependent and vulnerable
to walk its dusty streets,
to feel sorrow and heartache,
to be betrayed, bereft of friends,
to die on a cross, derided and forsaken,
to rise from the dead, victorious,
to bring us eternal life.
God of the Second Coming,
Judge of all the world,
your Son will reign as Prince of Peace.
He will make poverty and hunger cease
and end sorrow and death.
He will make new heavens and new earth.
When he comes in glory
may we be ready to meet him.

Ash Wednesday

'Remember that you are but dust
and to dust you shall return.'
Lord, forgive what I have been, amend what I am
and direct what I shall be.
As ashes make the sign of the cross on my forehead
as a sign of repentance,
so change my heart and my life
by the power of your Cross and Passion.

Pray without Ceasing

Maundy Thursday

Towel-girded Lord,
You knelt and washed your disciples' sweaty feet –
a menial task
yet outward sign
of a new commandment
to love one another.
Gird us with humility
that we may be willing
to cast aside our pride
and serve you in our sisters and brothers.

Good Friday

Lord Jesus, you bore the sins of the world
and took its suffering upon yourself.
You opened wide your arms on the Cross
for us, for the world, for me.
Forgive our continued sin –
both deliberate and unconscious.
Lead us back to yourself,
confront us with the Cross
and all that you sacrificed for each one of us.
Draw us to yourself – to resurrection glory
and to newness of life.

Easter Day

Risen Lord, you conquered death
when you rose from the grave,
you opened the way to eternal life for us.
Because you live, we too shall live.
May we with blessed Mary and all your saints
share in a joyful resurrection. Alleluia.

Prayers for Moveable Feasts

Ascension

Our risen and ascended King,
all glory is yours.
Empowered by your Spirit
send us out to proclaim the gospel
to every nation.
May we abide in your love
and follow you faithfully,
that finally at the last,
when our earthly pilgrimage is ended,
we may thither ascend
to where you have gone before us.

Pentecost

Spirit of God, fill us with power
as at Pentecost.
Widen our vision to see
new challenges.
Open our minds to a fresh outlook.
Open our hearts to the fullness of your grace,
and open our lives to your glory
that we may go out in your strength
to show your love to a broken world.